SURVEY OF LAW SCHOOL FACULTY & STAFF: TRENDS IN FUNDING FOR LEGAL RESEARCH & SCHOLARSHIP, 2020 EDITION

ISBN 978-1-57440-623-8

Table of Contents

THE QUESTIONNAIRE

1. Please give us the following contact information:

   A. Name:
   B. Organization:
   C. Title
   D. Email Address:

2. Academic Title

   A. Professor
   B. Assistant/Associate Professor
   C. Lecturer or Research Fellow
   D. Adjunct/Clinical Faculty
   E. Emeritus
   F. Other (please specify)

3. Age of survey respondent

   A. Under 30
   B. 30-39
   C. 40-49
   D. 50-59
   E. 60 or Over

4. Gender of the survey participant

   A. Male
   B. Female

5. Law school enrollment

6. Is your law school public or private?

   A. Public
   B. Private

7. In the past semester how many courses did you teach?

   A. None
   B. One
   C. Two
   D. More than Two

8. What percentage of your work time would you estimate is accounted for by applying for grants and seeking funding sources?

9. What is the value of all grants for legal and related research that you have received within the past five years?

10. How would you rate the office of research and grants at your law school (or your general university office if this is one that you deal with) on the following services?

	Poor	Fair	Acceptable	Good	Excellent	N/A
Knowledge of Sources of Grants for Legal Scholars						
Knowledge of Grant/Proposal Writing						
Knowledge of Available Fellowships						
Databases and other Resources to Search for Grant Sources						
Ability to Lobby for the Law School in University Funding Initiatives						

11. How do you rate the current environment for grant support for legal research funding?

    A. Poor
    B. Fair
    C. Acceptable
    D. Good
    E. Excellent

12. How do you rate what you expect will be the future environment for grant support for legal research funding over the next two years?

    A. Poor
    B. Fair
    C. Acceptable
    D. Good
    E. Excellent

13. What percentage of your research funding over the past five years has come from each of the following sources?

    A. U.S. Federal Government and its Agencies and Departments
    B. Your own University or Law School
    C. Private Sector Foundations, Non-profits or Companies
    D. All Other

14. In which subject areas and from which institutional sources do you feel that funding is likely to increase and in which areas is it likely to decline?

15. How many grants have you applied for within the past 12 months?

16. Have you ever done any of the following? (check all that apply)

    A. Checked the law library collection for information about legal research funding?
    B. Checked the general university library for information about legal research funding?
    C. Used a grants or funding database offered by the law library
    D. Used a grants or funding database offered by the general university library
    E. Used a grants or funding database offered by the research office of the law school or general university

17. What can your research office or library do to better assist you in searching for and obtaining grants to support your research?

18. What are some of the best or emerging sources of support for legal research funding?

INSTITUTIONAL AFFILIATIONS OF THE SURVEY PARTICIPANTS

Albany Law School
Boston University
Brandeis School of Law
BYU Law School
California Western School of Law
Campbell Law School
Chicago Kent College of Law
Columbia University
Cornell Law School
CUNY School of Law
Dalhousie University
Delaware Law Widener University
Drexel University
Duke Law School
Harvard Law School
Hofstra University Law School
Lewis and Clark Law School
Marquette University Law School
Mercer University School of Law
Michigan State University College of Law
Northeastern University School of Law
Notre Dame Law School
NYU School of Law
Oklahoma City University School of Law
OSU Moritz College of Law
Rutgers Law School
Santa Clara Law School
SCU Law School - Tech Edge
Suffolk University Law School
SUNY Buffalo School of Law
Temple University Beasley School of Law
Texas Tech University School of Law

The Ohio State University Moritz College of Law
Thomas Jefferson School of Law
UC Irvine School of Law
UCONN School of Law
UIC John Marshall Law School
University of Akron School of Law
University of Alabama School of Law
University of Baltimore
University of Denver Law School
University of Florida Law School
University of Georgia School of Law
University of Illinois College of Law
University of Louisville Law School
University of Maryland Carey School of Law
University of Miami School of Law
University of Michigan Law
University of Mississippi
University of Missouri
University of New Mexico School of Law
University of Oklahoma
University of Oregon School of Law
University of Pittsburgh
University of San Diego School of Law
University of Texas School of Law
UNLV Boyd School of Law
Vermont Law School
Villanova University School of law
Western Michigan University Thomas M. Cooley Law School
Widener University: Commonwealth Law School
William and Mary Law School

Characteristics of the Sample

Law school ranking

	#
Top 20	12
20 – 50	19
51 – 80	20
81 – 100	15
101 – 150	19
More than 150	11
Total	96

Academic Title

	#
Professor	52
Assistant/Associate Professor/Lecturer or Research Fellow	15
Adjunct/Clinical Faculty	14
Emeritus	7
Staff and Administration	8
Total	96

Age of survey respondent

	#
30-39	7
40-49	9
50-59	26
60 or Over	54
Total	96

Gender of the survey participant

	#
Male	59
Female	37
Total	96

Law school enrollment

	#
Less than 500	23
500 - 600	28
601 - 1000	26
More than 1000	19
Total	96

Is your law school public or private?

	#
Public	46
Private	50
Total	96

In the past semester how many courses did you teach?

	#
None	21
One	34
Two	31
More than Two	10
Total	96

SUMMARY OF MAIN FINDINGS

Work Time Accounted for by Applying for Grants and Seeking Funding Sources

We asked: What percentage of your work time would you estimate is accounted for by applying for grants and seeking funding sources?

The mean was 5.63% with a range of 0 to 35%. As might be expected, age was one of the best predictors, with the youngest faculty and staff, age 30-39 spending 16.67% of their time looking for funding. Females spend more time than men looking for funding, 7.53% vs. 4.33%.

Value of Grants Received in the Past Five Years

We asked: What is the value of all grants (in US $) for legal and related research that you have received within the past five years?

The median value of grants was $0 but the mean was $100,426 and one respondent reported $1.35 million. The general pattern was for a few respondents to report relatively high figures that account for most grants received. Some other large sums reported were: $1,000,000 $850,000, $600,000, and $500,000. Another interesting fact is that clinical and adjunct faculty, as well as staff and administration, were as active as regular faculty in obtaining research support, a different pattern than in many other fields. Female in the sample narrowly outraised the mean, attaining a mean of $105,038 vs. 97,571 for men. Higher ranking schools did not significantly outperform lower ranking ones, except those at the very end of the ranking scale, where funds raised fell off dramatically. Otherwise, funds raised were somewhat independent of academic reputation.

Assessment of the Office of Research and Grants' Knowledge of Sources for Grants for Legal Scholars

We asked: How would you rate the office of research and grants at your law school (or your general university office if this is one that you deal with) on the following services? For this series of questions we presented to respondents five possible answers – poor – fair – acceptable – good – excellent – and asked them to choose one.

First, we asked: How would you rate the office of research and grants at your law school on knowledge of sources of grants for legal scholars?

A little more than 32% did not answer and a plurality of 17.71% answered poor while only 10.42% answered excellent. The second most common answer was "acceptable" given by 15.63% of respondents. Views were highly impacted by law school rank, with half of those from schools in the top 20 answering "good" or "excellent" far higher than for other ranking cohorts. Females were unhappier than males with more than 40% choosing either "poor" or "fair" vs. only about 28% of males who felt the same way. Economies of scale may be an issue, as larger law schools tended to have more satisfied faculty and staff in this area than did smaller schools.

Assessment of the Office of Research and Grants' Knowledge of Grant Proposal Writing

Next, we asked: How would you rate the office of research and grants at your law school on knowledge of grant/proposal writing?

A shade more than 26% labelled their offices good or excellent while more than 31% considered them poor or fair. Satisfaction was much lower at lower than higher ranked law schools. Small schools, those with fewer than 500 students, fared particularly poorly with close to 35% considering school knowledge in the area to be poor or fail and about half this percentage considering it good or excellent.

Assessment of the Office of Research and Grants' Knowledge of Available Fellowships

Results were somewhat similar when we asked: How would you rate the office of research and grants at your law school on knowledge of available fellowships? A shade more than 24% considered knowledge to be good or excellent while more than 33% called it poor or fair. The difference between top 20 and other schools was vast, with 75% of those from top 20 schools choosing good or excellent. Also, law school size was again a big factor.

Assessment of the Office of Research and Grants' Offerings of Databases and other Resources to Search for Grants

Next, we asked: How would you rate the office of research and grants at your law school on databases and other resources to search for grant sources?

A plurality of 15.63% chose fair, and poor, the next most common answer, was chosen by 14.58% of respondents. A huge gender gap existed in this area: only a bit more than 8% of women felt that their schools were performing well in this area vs. more than 32% of men.

Assessment of the Office of Research and Grants' Ability to Lobby for the Law School in University Funding Initiatives

We asked: How would you rate the office of research and grants at your law school on the ability to lobby for the law school in university funding initiatives?

The most common answer was "fair", given by 15.63%; "acceptable" was the next most common answer, given by 13.54% of respondents.

Rating the Current Environment for Legal Research Funding

We asked: How do you rate the current environment for grant support for legal research funding?

"Fair" was the most common answer, given by 28.13% of respondents. Individuals from top 20 schools and those in staff and administration were the most likely to feel that the outlook for grants was good or excellent. Survey respondents who did not teaching or who taught only one course were more likely than those who taught two or more courses to feel that the outlook for grants was good or excellent.

View of the Probable Future Environment for Legal Research Spending

We asked: How do you rate what you expect will be the future environment for grant support for legal research funding over the next two years?

Results were similar to those for the same question probing the recent past. A plurality of 21.88% chose "fair" while the next most common answer – given by 21.88% -- was "acceptable."

Sources of Support for Legal Research Funding

We asked: What percentage of your research funding over the past five years has come from each of the following sources? We listed the 1) US Federal Government and its agencies and departments, 2) funding from the parent university or law school, private sector foundations, 3) non-profits or companies and finally, 4) all other sources.

US Federal Support for Legal Research Funding

The US Federal Government accounted for only 6.73% of total grants, but a much higher percentage – 14.43% -- for top 20 schools.

Respondents' own university or law school was the source of a mean of 43.32% of grant support, though the median was just 15% and the range 0 to 100%.

Professors and assistant professors dominated this funding and, for them, it accounted for at least half of total research funding. Public college law schools were also more dependent on this form of funding, accounting for 49.14% of all funding vs, only 37.32% for those from private college law schools.

Private Sector Support for Legal Research Funding

The private sector, including foundations and other non-profits and private companies, accounted for a mean of 16.38% of research funding. This form of funding was especially important for younger faculty and staff; for those from 30-39 years of age, private sector funding sources accounted for 68.67% of total funding. Also, it was important for women, accounting for 27.28% of funding vs. only 10.05% for men. Bigger schools tended to have more success than smaller ones; for respondents from schools with fewer than 500 students, private sector sources accounted for only 11.44% of total funding but for those with from 601-1,000 students, it was 21.56%. Respondents from private college law schools had more luck than those from public college law schools; for respondents form the former, private sector sources accounted for 20.54% of funding vs. only 11.97% for public colleges.

Other Funding Sources

All other funding sources accounted for 8.18% of total funding.

Number of Grants Applied for in the Past Year

We asked: How many grants have you applied for within the past 12 months?

The mean was 1.26 with a range of 0 to 12. Age was a big factor; the younger the faculty or staff member, the more grants that they have applied for in the past year. Those aged 30-39 applied for a mean of 3 grants in the past year with a median of 2 while those age 60 and over applied for a mean of 0.97 and a median of 0.

Use of Specific Law School and University Resources for Finding Legal Research Funding

We asked the respondents if they had used any specific resources of their university related to assistance in grant procurement. We asked about the following: 1) general information from the university law library about funding sources, 2) general information from the university library about research funding sources, 3) research funding online databases offered by the law library, 4) research funding online databases offered by the general university library, 5) research funding database offered by the research office of the law school or the general university.

Only 8,33% had used their law library collection to search for legal research funding; use of the law library for this purpose was highest among faculty at lower ranked law schools, for those ranked 100 or lower about 20% had used the law library for this this purpose. Much of the use was at private university law schools.

Only 4.17% had used the general university library for research into funding sources for legal research and scholarship. Older faculty, particularly emeritus faculty, were the most likely to use the general university library.

6.25% have used funding or grants databases available from the law library. The younger the faculty or staff member, the greater the likelihood of such use. Once again use was greatest at private college law schools.

11.46% have used a grants or funding database offered by the general university library. Almost all of this activity was at the top three tiers or law school ranking, from 1 to 80 in the rankings. Also, most of this use was at public university law schools, at which 19.57% of faculty and staff had used funding databases from the general university library; only 4% of those at private college law schools had done the same.

Also, 11.46% had used a grants or funding database offered by the research office of the law school or general university. Faculty and staff from law schools ranked 20 to 80 were the most common users. Once again, most use was by faculty and staff under age 50. Use was also twice as common among women than men; 16.22% of women in the sample had used the databases from the cited source vs. only 8.47% of men.

DATA AND RESPONSES TO OPEN ENDED QUESTIONS

Table 1.1 What percentage of your work time would you estimate is accounted for by applying for grants and seeking funding sources?

	Mean	Median	Minimum	Maximum
Entire sample	5.63	0.00	0.00	35.00

Table 1.2 What percentage of your work time would you estimate is accounted for by applying for grants and seeking funding sources? Broken out by law school ranking

Law school ranking	Mean	Median	Minimum	Maximum
Top 20	6.82	0.00	0.00	35.00
20 - 50	4.75	0.00	0.00	25.00
51 - 80	7.94	5.00	0.00	20.00
81 - 100	3.06	1.00	0.00	10.00
101 - 150	3.64	0.00	0.00	20.00
More than 150	7.43	0.00	0.00	30.00

Table 1.3 What percentage of your work time would you estimate is accounted for by applying for grants and seeking funding sources? Broken out by Academic Title

Academic Title	Mean	Median	Minimum	Maximum
Professor	4.73	0.50	0.00	20.00
Assistant/Associate Professor/Lecturer or Research Fellow	3.83	0.00	0.00	15.00
Adjunct/Clinical Faculty	8.89	0.00	0.00	35.00
Emeritus	5.00	0.00	0.00	20.00
Staff and Administration	10.29	2.00	0.00	30.00

Table 1.4 What percentage of your work time would you estimate is accounted for by applying for grants and seeking funding sources? Broken out by age of survey respondent

Age of survey respondent	Mean	Median	Minimum	Maximum
30-39	16.67	12.50	5.00	35.00
40-49	3.71	5.00	0.00	10.00
50-59	3.71	0.00	0.00	20.00
60 or Over	5.31	0.00	0.00	30.00

Table 1.5 What percentage of your work time would you estimate is accounted for by applying for grants and seeking funding sources? Broken out by gender of the survey participant

Gender of the survey participant	Mean	Median	Minimum	Maximum
Male	4.33	0.00	0.00	20.00
Female	7.53	5.00	0.00	35.00

Table 1.6 What percentage of your work time would you estimate is accounted for by applying for grants and seeking funding sources? Broken out by law school enrollment

Law school enrollment	Mean	Median	Minimum	Maximum
Less than 500	4.43	0.00	0.00	30.00
500 - 600	5.79	1.00	0.00	20.00
601 - 1000	6.75	5.00	0.00	25.00
More than 1000	5.07	0.00	0.00	35.00

Table 1.7 What percentage of your work time would you estimate is accounted for by applying for grants and seeking funding sources? Broken out for public and private universities

Is your law school public or private?	Mean	Median	Minimum	Maximum
Public	5.60	0.00	0.00	20.00
Private	5.65	1.00	0.00	35.00

Table 1.8 What percentage of your work time would you estimate is accounted for by applying for grants and seeking funding sources? Broken out by in the past semester how many courses did you teach?

In the past semester how many courses did you teach?	Mean	Median	Minimum	Maximum
None	8.07	1.50	0.00	30.00
One	5.25	0.00	0.00	35.00
Two	4.65	0.00	0.00	20.00
More than Two	5.75	0.50	0.00	20.00

Table 2.1 What is the value of all grants (in US $) for legal and related research that you have received within the past five years?

	Mean	Median	Minimum	Maximum
Entire sample	100426.47	0.00	0.00	1350000.00

Table 2.2 What is the value of all grants (in US $) for legal and related research that you have received within the past five years? Broken out by law school ranking

Law school ranking	Mean	Median	Minimum	Maximum
Top 20	101181.82	3000.00	0.00	850000.00
20 - 50	102857.14	0.00	0.00	1350000.00
51 - 80	149461.54	15000.00	0.00	600000.00
81 - 100	70500.00	2500.00	0.00	500000.00
101 - 150	120615.38	0.00	0.00	1000000.00
More than 150	8571.43	0.00	0.00	50000.00

Table 2.3 What is the value of all grants (in US $) for legal and related research that you have received within the past five years? Broken out by Academic Title

Academic Title	Mean	Median	Minimum	Maximum
Professor	84904.76	0.00	0.00	1000000.00
Assistant/Associate Professor/Lecturer or Research Fellow	36300.00	0.00	0.00	200000.00
Adjunct/Clinical Faculty	134285.71	0.00	0.00	850000.00
Emeritus	337500.00	0.00	0.00	1350000.00
Staff and Administration	122000.00	0.00	0.00	600000.00

Table 2.4 What is the value of all grants (in US $) for legal and related research that you have received within the past five years? Broken out by age of survey respondent

Age of survey respondent	Mean	Median	Minimum	Maximum
30-39	265750.00	105000.00	3000.00	850000.00
40-49	121428.57	25000.00	0.00	500000.00
50-59	118055.56	0.00	0.00	1000000.00
60 or Over	71564.10	0.00	0.00	1350000.00

Table 2.5 What is the value of all grants (in US $) for legal and related research that you have received within the past five years? Broken out by gender of the survey participant

Gender of the survey participant	Mean	Median	Minimum	Maximum
Male	97571.43	0.00	0.00	1350000.00
Female	105038.46	4000.00	0.00	850000.00

Table 2.6 What is the value of all grants (in US $) for legal and related research that you have received within the past five years? Broken out by law school enrollment

Law school enrollment	Mean	Median	Minimum	Maximum
Less than 500	15230.77	0.00	0.00	95000.00
500 - 600	183318.18	0.00	0.00	1350000.00
601 - 1000	56352.94	0.00	0.00	500000.00
More than 1000	102500.00	0.00	0.00	850000.00

Table 2.7 What is the value of all grants (in US $) for legal and related research that you have received within the past five years? Broken out for public and private universities

Is your law school public or private?	Mean	Median	Minimum	Maximum
Public	73366.67	0.00	0.00	1350000.00
Private	121789.47	0.00	0.00	1000000.00

Table 2.8 What is the value of all grants (in US $) for legal and related research that you have received within the past five years? Broken out by in the past semester how many courses did you teach?

In the past semester how many courses did you teach?	Mean	Median	Minimum	Maximum
None	126363.64	0.00	0.00	1350000.00
One	97291.67	0.00	0.00	850000.00
Two	65230.77	0.00	0.00	500000.00
More than Two	201142.86	8000.00	0.00	1000000.00

Table 3 How would you rate the office of research and grants at your law school (or your general university office if this is one that you deal with) on the following services?

Table 3.1.1 How would you rate the office of research and grants at your law school on knowledge of sources of grants for legal scholars?

	No Answer	Poor	Fair	Acceptable	Good	Excellent
Entire sample	32.29%	17.71%	14.58%	15.63%	9.38%	10.42%

Table 3.1.2 How would you rate the office of research and grants at your law school on knowledge of sources of grants for legal scholars? Broken out by law school ranking

Law school ranking	No Answer	Poor	Fair	Acceptable	Good	Excellent
Top 20	16.67%	8.33%	16.67%	8.33%	16.67%	33.33%
20 - 50	52.63%	10.53%	15.79%	0.00%	15.79%	5.26%
51 - 80	15.00%	15.00%	15.00%	30.00%	10.00%	15.00%
81 - 100	33.33%	13.33%	13.33%	33.33%	6.67%	0.00%
101 - 150	21.05%	36.84%	15.79%	10.53%	5.26%	10.53%
More than 150	63.64%	18.18%	9.09%	9.09%	0.00%	0.00%

Table 3.1.3 How would you rate the office of research and grants at your law school on knowledge of sources of grants for legal scholars? Broken out by Academic Title

Academic Title	No Answer	Poor	Fair	Acceptable	Good	Excellent
Professor	23.08%	26.92%	17.31%	15.38%	7.69%	9.62%
Assistant/Associate Professor/Lecturer or Research Fellow	46.67%	6.67%	6.67%	20.00%	13.33%	6.67%
Adjunct/Clinical Faculty	50.00%	0.00%	14.29%	7.14%	7.14%	21.43%
Emeritus	42.86%	28.57%	14.29%	14.29%	0.00%	0.00%
Staff and Administration	25.00%	0.00%	12.50%	25.00%	25.00%	12.50%

Table 3.1.4 How would you rate the office of research and grants at your law school on knowledge of sources of grants for legal scholars? Broken out by age of survey respondent

Age of survey respondent	No Answer	Poor	Fair	Acceptable	Good	Excellent
30-39	0.00%	0.00%	28.57%	42.86%	0.00%	28.57%
40-49	33.33%	0.00%	44.44%	22.22%	0.00%	0.00%
50-59	30.77%	30.77%	7.69%	7.69%	11.54%	11.54%
60 or Over	37.04%	16.67%	11.11%	14.81%	11.11%	9.26%

Table 3.1.5 How would you rate the office of research and grants at your law school on knowledge of sources of grants for legal scholars? Broken out by gender of the survey participant

Gender of the survey participant	No Answer	Poor	Fair	Acceptable	Good	Excellent
Male	33.90%	15.25%	11.86%	16.95%	10.17%	11.86%
Female	29.73%	21.62%	18.92%	13.51%	8.11%	8.11%

Table 3.1.6 How would you rate the office of research and grants at your law school on knowledge of sources of grants for legal scholars? Broken out by law school enrollment

Law school enrollment	No Answer	Poor	Fair	Acceptable	Good	Excellent
Less than 500	43.48%	26.09%	8.70%	13.04%	0.00%	8.70%
500 - 600	25.00%	14.29%	14.29%	25.00%	17.86%	3.57%
601 - 1000	30.77%	15.38%	15.38%	15.38%	11.54%	11.54%
More than 1000	31.58%	15.79%	21.05%	5.26%	5.26%	21.05%

Table 3.1.7 How would you rate the office of research and grants at your law school on knowledge of sources of grants for legal scholars? Broken out for public and private universities

Is your law school public or private?	No Answer	Poor	Fair	Acceptable	Good	Excellent
Public	28.26%	19.57%	8.70%	23.91%	6.52%	13.04%
Private	36.00%	16.00%	20.00%	8.00%	12.00%	8.00%

Table 3.1.8 How would you rate the office of research and grants at your law school on knowledge of sources of grants for legal scholars? Broken out by in the past semester how many courses did you teach?

In the past semester how many courses did you teach?	No Answer	Poor	Fair	Acceptable	Good	Excellent
None	33.33%	14.29%	19.05%	19.05%	4.76%	9.52%
One	41.18%	8.82%	14.71%	14.71%	5.88%	14.71%
Two	29.03%	29.03%	9.68%	16.13%	9.68%	6.45%
More than Two	10.00%	20.00%	20.00%	10.00%	30.00%	10.00%

Table 3.2.1 How would you rate the office of research and grants at your law school on knowledge of grant/proposal writing?

	No Answer	Poor	Fair	Acceptable	Good	Excellent
Entire sample	31.25%	15.63%	15.63%	11.46%	14.58%	11.46%

Table 3.2.2 How would you rate the office of research and grants at your law school on knowledge of grant/proposal writing? Broken out by law school ranking

Law school ranking	No Answer	Poor	Fair	Acceptable	Good	Excellent
Top 20	16.67%	0.00%	16.67%	16.67%	25.00%	25.00%
20 - 50	47.37%	5.26%	21.05%	5.26%	10.53%	10.53%
51 - 80	20.00%	15.00%	10.00%	15.00%	25.00%	15.00%
81 - 100	33.33%	20.00%	13.33%	20.00%	6.67%	6.67%
101 - 150	21.05%	26.32%	21.05%	5.26%	15.79%	10.53%
More than 150	54.55%	27.27%	9.09%	9.09%	0.00%	0.00%

Table 3.2.3 How would you rate the office of research and grants at your law school on knowledge of grant/proposal writing? Broken out by Academic Title

Academic Title	No Answer	Poor	Fair	Acceptable	Good	Excellent
Professor	23.08%	23.08%	15.38%	11.54%	15.38%	11.54%
Assistant/Associate Professor/Lecturer or Research Fellow	46.67%	6.67%	13.33%	6.67%	20.00%	6.67%
Adjunct/Clinical Faculty	42.86%	0.00%	14.29%	14.29%	7.14%	21.43%
Emeritus	42.86%	14.29%	28.57%	14.29%	0.00%	0.00%
Staff and Administration	25.00%	12.50%	12.50%	12.50%	25.00%	12.50%

Table 3.2.4 How would you rate the office of research and grants at your law school on knowledge of grant/proposal writing? Broken out by age of survey respondent

Age of survey respondent	No Answer	Poor	Fair	Acceptable	Good	Excellent
30-39	0.00%	0.00%	42.86%	14.29%	14.29%	28.57%
40-49	33.33%	0.00%	22.22%	11.11%	33.33%	0.00%
50-59	26.92%	26.92%	7.69%	3.85%	11.54%	23.08%
60 or Over	37.04%	14.81%	14.81%	14.81%	12.96%	5.56%

Table 3.2.5 How would you rate the office of research and grants at your law school on knowledge of grant/proposal writing? Broken out by gender of the survey participant

Gender of the survey participant	No Answer	Poor	Fair	Acceptable	Good	Excellent
Male	30.51%	13.56%	11.86%	13.56%	16.95%	13.56%
Female	32.43%	18.92%	21.62%	8.11%	10.81%	8.11%

Table 3.2.6 How would you rate the office of research and grants at your law school on knowledge of grant/proposal writing? Broken out by law school enrollment

Law school enrollment	No Answer	Poor	Fair	Acceptable	Good	Excellent
Less than 500	34.78%	26.09%	8.70%	13.04%	8.70%	8.70%
500 - 600	25.00%	10.71%	17.86%	14.29%	25.00%	7.14%
601 - 1000	34.62%	15.38%	11.54%	11.54%	15.38%	11.54%
More than 1000	31.58%	10.53%	26.32%	5.26%	5.26%	21.05%

Table 3.2.7 How would you rate the office of research and grants at your law school on knowledge of grant/proposal writing? Broken out for public and private universities

Is your law school public or private?	No Answer	Poor	Fair	Acceptable	Good	Excellent
Public	30.43%	10.87%	19.57%	13.04%	15.22%	10.87%
Private	32.00%	20.00%	12.00%	10.00%	14.00%	12.00%

Table 3.2.8 How would you rate the office of research and grants at your law school on knowledge of grant/proposal writing? Broken out by in the past semester how many courses did you teach?

In the past semester how many courses did you teach?	No Answer	Poor	Fair	Acceptable	Good	Excellent
None	33.33%	14.29%	23.81%	14.29%	9.52%	4.76%
One	38.24%	8.82%	11.76%	8.82%	11.76%	20.59%
Two	29.03%	22.58%	12.90%	12.90%	16.13%	6.45%
More than Two	10.00%	20.00%	20.00%	10.00%	30.00%	10.00%

Table 3.3.1 How would you rate the office of research and grants at your law school on knowledge of available fellowships?

	No Answer	Poor	Fair	Acceptable	Good	Excellent
Entire sample	30.21%	17.71%	15.63%	12.50%	12.50%	11.46%

Table 3.3.2 How would you rate the office of research and grants at your law school on knowledge of available fellowships? Broken out by law school ranking

Law school ranking	No Answer	Poor	Fair	Acceptable	Good	Excellent
Top 20	8.33%	8.33%	0.00%	8.33%	25.00%	50.00%
20 - 50	47.37%	5.26%	15.79%	10.53%	15.79%	5.26%
51 - 80	25.00%	15.00%	20.00%	15.00%	15.00%	10.00%
81 - 100	26.67%	20.00%	13.33%	26.67%	6.67%	6.67%
101 - 150	21.05%	31.58%	26.32%	5.26%	10.53%	5.26%
More than 150	54.55%	27.27%	9.09%	9.09%	0.00%	0.00%

Table 3.3.3 How would you rate the office of research and grants at your law school on knowledge of available fellowships? Broken out by Academic Title

Academic Title	No Answer	Poor	Fair	Acceptable	Good	Excellent
Professor	19.23%	26.92%	19.23%	13.46%	13.46%	7.69%
Assistant/Associate Professor/Lecturer or Research Fellow	53.33%	6.67%	13.33%	13.33%	6.67%	6.67%
Adjunct/Clinical Faculty	42.86%	0.00%	7.14%	0.00%	14.29%	35.71%
Emeritus	28.57%	14.29%	14.29%	28.57%	0.00%	14.29%
Staff and Administration	37.50%	12.50%	12.50%	12.50%	25.00%	0.00%

Table 3.3.4 How would you rate the office of research and grants at your law school on knowledge of available fellowships? Broken out by age of survey respondent

Age of survey respondent	No Answer	Poor	Fair	Acceptable	Good	Excellent
30-39	14.29%	0.00%	28.57%	14.29%	0.00%	42.86%
40-49	33.33%	0.00%	33.33%	33.33%	0.00%	0.00%
50-59	30.77%	26.92%	11.54%	7.69%	11.54%	11.54%
60 or Over	31.48%	18.52%	12.96%	11.11%	16.67%	9.26%

Table 3.3.5 How would you rate the office of research and grants at your law school on knowledge of available fellowships? Broken out by gender of the survey participant

Gender of the survey participant	No Answer	Poor	Fair	Acceptable	Good	Excellent
Male	30.51%	15.25%	13.56%	11.86%	15.25%	13.56%
Female	29.73%	21.62%	18.92%	13.51%	8.11%	8.11%

Table 3.3.6 How would you rate the office of research and grants at your law school on knowledge of available fellowships? Broken out by law school enrollment

Law school enrollment	No Answer	Poor	Fair	Acceptable	Good	Excellent
Less than 500	30.43%	34.78%	13.04%	8.70%	4.35%	8.70%
500 - 600	32.14%	10.71%	21.43%	14.29%	17.86%	3.57%
601 - 1000	30.77%	15.38%	11.54%	19.23%	11.54%	11.54%
More than 1000	26.32%	10.53%	15.79%	5.26%	15.79%	26.32%

Table 3.3.7 How would you rate the office of research and grants at your law school on knowledge of available fellowships? Broken out for public and private universities

Is your law school public or private?	No Answer	Poor	Fair	Acceptable	Good	Excellent
Public	28.26%	13.04%	19.57%	15.22%	10.87%	13.04%
Private	32.00%	22.00%	12.00%	10.00%	14.00%	10.00%

Table 3.3.8 How would you rate the office of research and grants at your law school on knowledge of available fellowships? Broken out by in the past semester how many courses did you teach?

In the past semester how many courses did you teach?	No Answer	Poor	Fair	Acceptable	Good	Excellent
None	33.33%	14.29%	19.05%	14.29%	9.52%	9.52%
One	38.24%	11.76%	8.82%	11.76%	5.88%	23.53%
Two	25.81%	25.81%	19.35%	9.68%	16.13%	3.23%
More than Two	10.00%	20.00%	20.00%	20.00%	30.00%	0.00%

Table 3.4.1 How would you rate the office of research and grants at your law school on databases and other resources to search for grant sources?

	No Answer	Poor	Fair	Acceptable	Good	Excellent
Entire sample	37.50%	14.58%	15.63%	9.38%	13.54%	9.38%

Table 3.4.2 How would you rate the office of research and grants at your law school on databases and other resources to search for grant sources? Broken out by law school ranking

Law school ranking	No Answer	Poor	Fair	Acceptable	Good	Excellent
Top 20	25.00%	0.00%	8.33%	16.67%	16.67%	33.33%
20 - 50	63.16%	0.00%	10.53%	15.79%	5.26%	5.26%
51 - 80	20.00%	15.00%	20.00%	5.00%	25.00%	15.00%
81 - 100	33.33%	13.33%	13.33%	20.00%	20.00%	0.00%
101 - 150	26.32%	31.58%	26.32%	0.00%	10.53%	5.26%
More than 150	63.64%	27.27%	9.09%	0.00%	0.00%	0.00%

Table 3.4.3 How would you rate the office of research and grants at your law school on databases and other resources to search for grant sources? Broken out by Academic Title

Academic Title	No Answer	Poor	Fair	Acceptable	Good	Excellent
Professor	30.77%	19.23%	17.31%	7.69%	17.31%	7.69%
Assistant/Associate Professor/Lecturer or Research Fellow	53.33%	13.33%	20.00%	6.67%	0.00%	6.67%
Adjunct/Clinical Faculty	50.00%	0.00%	0.00%	21.43%	7.14%	21.43%
Emeritus	28.57%	14.29%	14.29%	14.29%	28.57%	0.00%
Staff and Administration	37.50%	12.50%	25.00%	0.00%	12.50%	12.50%

Table 3.4.4 How would you rate the office of research and grants at your law school on databases and other resources to search for grant sources? Broken out by age of survey respondent

Age of survey respondent	No Answer	Poor	Fair	Acceptable	Good	Excellent
30-39	14.29%	0.00%	28.57%	28.57%	0.00%	28.57%
40-49	33.33%	0.00%	33.33%	11.11%	22.22%	0.00%
50-59	34.62%	26.92%	11.54%	3.85%	15.38%	7.69%
60 or Over	42.59%	12.96%	12.96%	9.26%	12.96%	9.26%

Table 3.4.5 How would you rate the office of research and grants at your law school on databases and other resources to search for grant sources? Broken out by gender of the survey participant

Gender of the survey participant	No Answer	Poor	Fair	Acceptable	Good	Excellent
Male	38.98%	11.86%	13.56%	3.39%	20.34%	11.86%
Female	35.14%	18.92%	18.92%	18.92%	2.70%	5.41%

Table 3.4.6 How would you rate the office of research and grants at your law school on databases and other resources to search for grant sources? Broken out by law school enrollment

Law school enrollment	No Answer	Poor	Fair	Acceptable	Good	Excellent
Less than 500	47.83%	26.09%	8.70%	8.70%	0.00%	8.70%
500 - 600	35.71%	10.71%	28.57%	0.00%	21.43%	3.57%
601 - 1000	34.62%	15.38%	7.69%	15.38%	15.38%	11.54%
More than 1000	31.58%	5.26%	15.79%	15.79%	15.79%	15.79%

Table 3.4.7 How would you rate the office of research and grants at your law school on databases and other resources to search for grant sources? Broken out for public and private universities

Is your law school public or private?	No Answer	Poor	Fair	Acceptable	Good	Excellent
Public	34.78%	13.04%	19.57%	8.70%	10.87%	13.04%
Private	40.00%	16.00%	12.00%	10.00%	16.00%	6.00%

Table 3.4.8 How would you rate the office of research and grants at your law school on databases and other resources to search for grant sources? Broken out by in the past semester how many courses did you teach?

In the past semester how many courses did you teach?	No Answer	Poor	Fair	Acceptable	Good	Excellent
None	38.10%	9.52%	23.81%	9.52%	9.52%	9.52%
One	38.24%	11.76%	5.88%	11.76%	17.65%	14.71%
Two	41.94%	19.35%	16.13%	9.68%	9.68%	3.23%
More than Two	20.00%	20.00%	30.00%	0.00%	20.00%	10.00%

Table 3.5.1 How would you rate the office of research and grants at your law school on the ability to lobby for the law school in university funding initiatives?

	No Answer	Poor	Fair	Acceptable	Good	Excellent
Entire sample	41.67%	11.46%	15.63%	13.54%	7.29%	10.42%

Table 3.5.2 How would you rate the office of research and grants at your law school on the ability to lobby for the law school in university funding initiatives? Broken out by law school ranking

Law school ranking	No Answer	Poor	Fair	Acceptable	Good	Excellent
Top 20	16.67%	16.67%	0.00%	8.33%	25.00%	33.33%
20 - 50	63.16%	5.26%	15.79%	5.26%	5.26%	5.26%
51 - 80	20.00%	10.00%	20.00%	25.00%	5.00%	20.00%
81 - 100	46.67%	20.00%	6.67%	26.67%	0.00%	0.00%
101 - 150	36.84%	15.79%	21.05%	10.53%	10.53%	5.26%
More than 150	72.73%	0.00%	27.27%	0.00%	0.00%	0.00%

Table 3.5.3 How would you rate the office of research and grants at your law school on the ability to lobby for the law school in university funding initiatives? Broken out by Academic Title

Academic Title	No Answer	Poor	Fair	Acceptable	Good	Excellent
Professor	36.54%	15.38%	17.31%	17.31%	5.77%	7.69%
Assistant/Associate Professor/Lecturer or Research Fellow	60.00%	6.67%	13.33%	6.67%	6.67%	6.67%
Adjunct/Clinical Faculty	50.00%	14.29%	7.14%	0.00%	7.14%	21.43%
Emeritus	42.86%	0.00%	14.29%	28.57%	14.29%	0.00%
Staff and Administration	25.00%	0.00%	25.00%	12.50%	12.50%	25.00%

Table 3.5.4 How would you rate the office of research and grants at your law school on the ability to lobby for the law school in university funding initiatives? Broken out by age of survey respondent

Age of survey respondent	No Answer	Poor	Fair	Acceptable	Good	Excellent
30-39	14.29%	14.29%	28.57%	14.29%	0.00%	28.57%
40-49	44.44%	0.00%	22.22%	33.33%	0.00%	0.00%
50-59	42.31%	15.38%	19.23%	3.85%	7.69%	11.54%
60 or Over	44.44%	11.11%	11.11%	14.81%	9.26%	9.26%

Table 3.5.5 How would you rate the office of research and grants at your law school on the ability to lobby for the law school in university funding initiatives? Broken out by gender of the survey participant

Gender of the survey participant	No Answer	Poor	Fair	Acceptable	Good	Excellent
Male	40.68%	10.17%	13.56%	15.25%	8.47%	11.86%
Female	43.24%	13.51%	18.92%	10.81%	5.41%	8.11%

Table 3.5.6 How would you rate the office of research and grants at your law school on the ability to lobby for the law school in university funding initiatives? Broken out by law school enrollment

Law school enrollment	No Answer	Poor	Fair	Acceptable	Good	Excellent
Less than 500	43.48%	8.70%	21.74%	13.04%	4.35%	8.70%
500 - 600	46.43%	3.57%	21.43%	14.29%	7.14%	7.14%
601 - 1000	38.46%	19.23%	7.69%	19.23%	7.69%	7.69%
More than 1000	36.84%	15.79%	10.53%	5.26%	10.53%	21.05%

Table 3.5.7 How would you rate the office of research and grants at your law school on the ability to lobby for the law school in university funding initiatives? Broken out for public and private universities

Is your law school public or private?	No Answer	Poor	Fair	Acceptable	Good	Excellent
Public	36.96%	6.52%	15.22%	19.57%	8.70%	13.04%
Private	46.00%	16.00%	16.00%	8.00%	6.00%	8.00%

Table 3.5.8 How would you rate the office of research and grants at your law school on the ability to lobby for the law school in university funding initiatives? Broken out by in the past semester how many courses did you teach?

In the past semester how many courses did you teach?	No Answer	Poor	Fair	Acceptable	Good	Excellent
None	42.86%	0.00%	23.81%	14.29%	4.76%	14.29%
One	44.12%	11.76%	8.82%	11.76%	5.88%	17.65%
Two	41.94%	12.90%	19.35%	12.90%	9.68%	3.23%
More than Two	30.00%	30.00%	10.00%	20.00%	10.00%	0.00%

Table 4.1 How do you rate the current environment for grant support for legal research funding?

	No Answer	Poor	Fair	Acceptable	Good	Excellent
Entire sample	7.29%	20.83%	28.13%	20.83%	14.58%	8.33%

Table 4.2 How do you rate the current environment for grant support for legal research funding? Broken out by law school ranking

Law school ranking	No Answer	Poor	Fair	Acceptable	Good	Excellent
Top 20	8.33%	8.33%	8.33%	16.67%	41.67%	16.67%
20 - 50	15.79%	10.53%	26.32%	26.32%	5.26%	15.79%
51 - 80	0.00%	15.00%	30.00%	30.00%	25.00%	0.00%
81 - 100	6.67%	20.00%	33.33%	26.67%	6.67%	6.67%
101 - 150	5.26%	31.58%	42.11%	10.53%	10.53%	0.00%
More than 150	9.09%	45.45%	18.18%	9.09%	0.00%	18.18%

Table 4.3 How do you rate the current environment for grant support for legal research funding? Broken out by Academic Title

Academic Title	No Answer	Poor	Fair	Acceptable	Good	Excellent
Professor	5.77%	25.00%	38.46%	17.31%	7.69%	5.77%
Assistant/Associate Professor/Lecturer or Research Fellow	6.67%	20.00%	20.00%	33.33%	20.00%	0.00%
Adjunct/Clinical Faculty	21.43%	0.00%	7.14%	28.57%	21.43%	21.43%
Emeritus	0.00%	42.86%	28.57%	14.29%	0.00%	14.29%
Staff and Administration	0.00%	12.50%	12.50%	12.50%	50.00%	12.50%

Table 4.4 How do you rate the current environment for grant support for legal research funding? Broken out by age of survey respondent

Age of survey respondent	No Answer	Poor	Fair	Acceptable	Good	Excellent
30-39	0.00%	0.00%	14.29%	42.86%	42.86%	0.00%
40-49	0.00%	0.00%	66.67%	11.11%	11.11%	11.11%
50-59	7.69%	34.62%	23.08%	11.54%	15.38%	7.69%
60 or Over	9.26%	20.37%	25.93%	24.07%	11.11%	9.26%

Table 4.5 How do you rate the current environment for grant support for legal research funding? Broken out by gender of the survey participant

Gender of the survey participant	No Answer	Poor	Fair	Acceptable	Good	Excellent
Male	6.78%	15.25%	27.12%	28.81%	10.17%	11.86%
Female	8.11%	29.73%	29.73%	8.11%	21.62%	2.70%

Table 4.6 How do you rate the current environment for grant support for legal research funding? Broken out by law school enrollment

Law school enrollment	No Answer	Poor	Fair	Acceptable	Good	Excellent
Less than 500	13.04%	21.74%	30.43%	13.04%	13.04%	8.70%
500 - 600	0.00%	21.43%	32.14%	25.00%	10.71%	10.71%
601 - 1000	7.69%	26.92%	30.77%	15.38%	19.23%	0.00%
More than 1000	10.53%	10.53%	15.79%	31.58%	15.79%	15.79%

Table 4.7 How do you rate the current environment for grant support for legal research funding? Broken out for public and private universities

Is your law school public or private?	No Answer	Poor	Fair	Acceptable	Good	Excellent
Public	6.52%	15.22%	30.43%	28.26%	13.04%	6.52%
Private	8.00%	26.00%	26.00%	14.00%	16.00%	10.00%

Table 4.8 How do you rate the current environment for grant support for legal research funding? Broken out by in the past semester how many courses did you teach?

In the past semester how many courses did you teach?	No Answer	Poor	Fair	Acceptable	Good	Excellent
None	4.76%	23.81%	23.81%	19.05%	9.52%	19.05%
One	14.71%	14.71%	20.59%	23.53%	20.59%	5.88%
Two	0.00%	25.81%	32.26%	22.58%	12.90%	6.45%
More than Two	10.00%	20.00%	50.00%	10.00%	10.00%	0.00%

Table 5.1 How do you rate what you expect will be the future environment for grant support for legal research funding over the next two years?

	No Answer	Poor	Fair	Acceptable	Good	Excellent
Entire sample	8.33%	18.75%	28.13%	21.88%	14.58%	8.33%

Table 5.2 How do you rate what you expect will be the future environment for grant support for legal research funding over the next two years? Broken out by law school ranking

Law school ranking	No Answer	Poor	Fair	Acceptable	Good	Excellent
Top 20	8.33%	8.33%	8.33%	16.67%	41.67%	16.67%
20 - 50	15.79%	5.26%	36.84%	26.32%	10.53%	5.26%
51 - 80	0.00%	15.00%	20.00%	35.00%	20.00%	10.00%
81 - 100	6.67%	20.00%	33.33%	26.67%	0.00%	13.33%
101 - 150	5.26%	31.58%	36.84%	10.53%	15.79%	0.00%
More than 150	18.18%	36.36%	27.27%	9.09%	0.00%	9.09%

Table 5.3 How do you rate what you expect will be the future environment for grant support for legal research funding over the next two years? Broken out by Academic Title

Academic Title	No Answer	Poor	Fair	Acceptable	Good	Excellent
Professor	7.69%	23.08%	34.62%	21.15%	7.69%	5.77%
Assistant/Associate Professor/Lecturer or Research Fellow	6.67%	20.00%	13.33%	26.67%	26.67%	6.67%
Adjunct/Clinical Faculty	21.43%	0.00%	14.29%	35.71%	14.29%	14.29%
Emeritus	0.00%	28.57%	42.86%	14.29%	14.29%	0.00%
Staff and Administration	0.00%	12.50%	25.00%	0.00%	37.50%	25.00%

Table 5.4 How do you rate what you expect will be the future environment for grant support for legal research funding over the next two years? Broken out by age of survey respondent

Age of survey respondent	No Answer	Poor	Fair	Acceptable	Good	Excellent
30-39	0.00%	0.00%	14.29%	14.29%	57.14%	14.29%
40-49	11.11%	0.00%	55.56%	11.11%	22.22%	0.00%
50-59	7.69%	30.77%	23.08%	15.38%	7.69%	15.38%
60 or Over	9.26%	18.52%	27.78%	27.78%	11.11%	5.56%

Table 5.5 How do you rate what you expect will be the future environment for grant support for legal research funding over the next two years? Broken out by gender of the survey participant

Gender of the survey participant	No Answer	Poor	Fair	Acceptable	Good	Excellent
Male	6.78%	15.25%	28.81%	28.81%	8.47%	11.86%
Female	10.81%	24.32%	27.03%	10.81%	24.32%	2.70%

Table 5.6 How do you rate what you expect will be the future environment for grant support for legal research funding over the next two years? Broken out by law school enrollment

Law school enrollment	No Answer	Poor	Fair	Acceptable	Good	Excellent
Less than 500	13.04%	21.74%	30.43%	13.04%	17.39%	4.35%
500 - 600	0.00%	21.43%	25.00%	28.57%	10.71%	14.29%
601 - 1000	7.69%	23.08%	34.62%	15.38%	15.38%	3.85%
More than 1000	15.79%	5.26%	21.05%	31.58%	15.79%	10.53%

Table 5.7 How do you rate what you expect will be the future environment for grant support for legal research funding over the next two years? Broken out for public and private universities

Is your law school public or private?	No Answer	Poor	Fair	Acceptable	Good	Excellent
Public	6.52%	13.04%	26.09%	34.78%	13.04%	6.52%
Private	10.00%	24.00%	30.00%	10.00%	16.00%	10.00%

Table 5.8 How do you rate what you expect will be the future environment for grant support for legal research funding over the next two years? Broken out by in the past semester how many courses did you teach?

In the past semester how many courses did you teach?	No Answer	Poor	Fair	Acceptable	Good	Excellent
None	4.76%	14.29%	38.10%	14.29%	19.05%	9.52%
One	14.71%	14.71%	23.53%	20.59%	14.71%	11.76%
Two	3.23%	25.81%	25.81%	25.81%	12.90%	6.45%
More than Two	10.00%	20.00%	30.00%	30.00%	10.00%	0.00%

Table 6 What percentage of your research funding over the past five years has come from each of the following sources?

Table 6.1.1 What percentage of your research funding over the past five years has come from U.S. Federal government and its agencies and departments?

	Mean	Median	Minimum	Maximum
Entire sample	6.73	0.00	0.00	100.00

Table 6.1.2 What percentage of your research funding over the past five years has come from U.S. Federal government and its agencies and departments? Broken out by law school ranking

Law school ranking	Mean	Median	Minimum	Maximum
Top 20	14.43	0.00	0.00	100.00
20 - 50	0.00	0.00	0.00	0.00
51 - 80	7.00	0.00	0.00	50.00
81 - 100	10.00	0.00	0.00	100.00
101 - 150	9.55	0.00	0.00	55.00
More than 150	0.00	0.00	0.00	0.00

Table 6.1.3 What percentage of your research funding over the past five years has come from U.S. Federal government and its agencies and departments? Broken out by Academic Title

Academic Title	Mean	Median	Minimum	Maximum
Professor	4.08	0.00	0.00	50.00
Assistant/Associate Professor/Lecturer or Research Fellow	5.00	0.00	0.00	55.00
Adjunct/Clinical Faculty	14.29	0.00	0.00	100.00
Emeritus	16.67	0.00	0.00	100.00
Staff and Administration	8.33	0.00	0.00	25.00

Table 6.1.4 What percentage of your research funding over the past five years has come from U.S. Federal government and its agencies and departments? Broken out by age of survey respondent

Age of survey respondent	Mean	Median	Minimum	Maximum
30-39	13.75	0.00	0.00	55.00
40-49	5.00	0.00	0.00	20.00
50-59	5.25	0.00	0.00	50.00
60 or Over	6.97	0.00	0.00	100.00

Table 6.1.5 What percentage of your research funding over the past five years has come from U.S. Federal government and its agencies and departments? Broken out by gender of the survey participant

Gender of the survey participant	Mean	Median	Minimum	Maximum
Male	7.95	0.00	0.00	100.00
Female	4.57	0.00	0.00	55.00

Table 6.1.6 What percentage of your research funding over the past five years has come from U.S. Federal government and its agencies and departments? Broken out by law school enrollment

Law school enrollment	Mean	Median	Minimum	Maximum
Less than 500	10.33	0.00	0.00	100.00
500 - 600	5.43	0.00	0.00	50.00
601 - 1000	1.54	0.00	0.00	20.00
More than 1000	10.08	0.00	0.00	100.00

Table 6.1.7 What percentage of your research funding over the past five years has come from U.S. Federal government and its agencies and departments? Broken out for public and private universities

Is your law school public or private?	Mean	Median	Minimum	Maximum
Public	7.73	0.00	0.00	100.00
Private	5.68	0.00	0.00	50.00

Table 6.1.8 What percentage of your research funding over the past five years has come from U.S. Federal government and its agencies and departments? Broken out by in the past semester how many courses did you teach?

In the past semester how many courses did you teach?	Mean	Median	Minimum	Maximum
None	14.09	0.00	0.00	100.00
One	6.64	0.00	0.00	100.00
Two	3.33	0.00	0.00	50.00
More than Two	7.14	0.00	0.00	50.00

Table 6.2.1 What percentage of your research funding over the past five years has come from your own university or law school?

	Mean	Median	Minimum	Maximum
Entire sample	43.32	15.00	0.00	100.00

Table 6.2.2 What percentage of your research funding over the past five years has come from your own university or law school? Broken out by law school ranking

Law school ranking	Mean	Median	Minimum	Maximum
Top 20	55.67	33.00	0.00	100.00
20 - 50	21.21	0.00	0.00	100.00
51 - 80	61.56	85.00	0.00	100.00
81 - 100	42.27	15.00	0.00	100.00
101 - 150	29.25	0.50	0.00	100.00
More than 150	55.71	90.00	0.00	100.00

Table 6.2.3 What percentage of your research funding over the past five years has come from your own university or law school? Broken out by Academic Title

Academic Title	Mean	Median	Minimum	Maximum
Professor	54.49	75.00	0.00	100.00
Assistant/Associate Professor/Lecturer or Research Fellow	50.00	50.00	0.00	100.00
Adjunct/Clinical Faculty	5.50	0.00	0.00	33.00
Emeritus	28.71	0.00	0.00	100.00
Staff and Administration	3.33	0.00	0.00	10.00

Table 6.2.4 What percentage of your research funding over the past five years has come from your own university or law school? Broken out by age of survey respondent

Age of survey respondent	Mean	Median	Minimum	Maximum
30-39	59.50	66.50	5.00	100.00
40-49	71.25	92.50	0.00	100.00
50-59	35.00	1.00	0.00	100.00
60 or Over	42.88	20.00	0.00	100.00

Table 6.2.5 What percentage of your research funding over the past five years has come from your own university or law school? Broken out by gender of the survey participant

Gender of the survey participant	Mean	Median	Minimum	Maximum
Male	39.32	10.00	0.00	100.00
Female	50.36	33.00	0.00	100.00

Table 6.2.6 What percentage of your research funding over the past five years has come from your own university or law school? Broken out by law school enrollment

Law school enrollment	Mean	Median	Minimum	Maximum
Less than 500	38.13	0.00	0.00	100.00
500 - 600	35.87	1.00	0.00	100.00
601 - 1000	55.94	70.00	0.00	100.00
More than 1000	45.79	33.00	0.00	100.00

Table 6.2.7 What percentage of your research funding over the past five years has come from your own university or law school? Broken out for public and private universities

Is your law school public or private?	Mean	Median	Minimum	Maximum
Public	49.14	50.00	0.00	100.00
Private	37.32	12.50	0.00	100.00

Table 6.2.8 What percentage of your research funding over the past five years has come from your own university or law school? Broken out by in the past semester how many courses did you teach?

In the past semester how many courses did you teach?	Mean	Median	Minimum	Maximum
None	29.69	0.00	0.00	100.00
One	43.22	33.00	0.00	100.00
Two	53.80	90.00	0.00	100.00
More than Two	33.00	8.00	0.00	100.00

Table 6.3.1 What percentage of your research funding over the past five years has come from private sector foundations, non-profits or companies?

	Mean	Median	Minimum	Maximum
Entire sample	16.38	0.00	0.00	100.00

Table 6.3.2 What percentage of your research funding over the past five years has come from private sector foundations, non-profits or companies? Broken out by law school ranking

Law school ranking	Mean	Median	Minimum	Maximum
Top 20	20.29	1.00	0.00	70.00
20 - 50	26.93	0.00	0.00	100.00
51 - 80	12.00	0.00	0.00	65.00
81 - 100	5.75	0.00	0.00	40.00
101 - 150	24.92	2.50	0.00	100.00
More than 150	2.86	0.00	0.00	10.00

Table 6.3.3 What percentage of your research funding over the past five years has come from private sector foundations, non-profits or companies? Broken out by Academic Title

Academic Title	Mean	Median	Minimum	Maximum
Professor	15.34	0.00	0.00	100.00
Assistant/Associate Professor/Lecturer or Research Fellow	16.11	0.00	0.00	100.00
Adjunct/Clinical Faculty	20.75	0.00	0.00	100.00
Emeritus	16.50	0.00	0.00	99.00
Staff and Administration	18.75	5.00	0.00	65.00

Table 6.3.4 What percentage of your research funding over the past five years has come from private sector foundations, non-profits or companies? Broken out by age of survey respondent

Age of survey respondent	Mean	Median	Minimum	Maximum
30-39	68.67	66.00	40.00	100.00
40-49	26.00	10.00	0.00	75.00
50-59	20.00	0.00	0.00	100.00
60 or Over	9.71	0.00	0.00	100.00

Table 6.3.5 What percentage of your research funding over the past five years has come from private sector foundations, non-profits or companies? Broken out by gender of the survey participant

Gender of the survey participant	Mean	Median	Minimum	Maximum
Male	10.05	0.00	0.00	100.00
Female	27.28	5.00	0.00	100.00

Table 6.3.6 What percentage of your research funding over the past five years has come from private sector foundations, non-profits or companies? Broken out by law school enrollment

Law school enrollment	Mean	Median	Minimum	Maximum
Less than 500	11.44	0.00	0.00	100.00
500 - 600	14.73	0.00	0.00	99.00
601 - 1000	21.56	0.00	0.00	100.00
More than 1000	18.71	0.50	0.00	100.00

Table 6.3.7 What percentage of your research funding over the past five years has come from private sector foundations, non-profits or companies? Broken out for public and private universities

Is your law school public or private?	Mean	Median	Minimum	Maximum
Public	11.97	0.00	0.00	100.00
Private	20.54	0.00	0.00	100.00

Table 6.3.8 What percentage of your research funding over the past five years has come from private sector foundations, non-profits or companies? Broken out by in the past semester how many courses did you teach?

In the past semester how many courses did you teach?	Mean	Median	Minimum	Maximum
None	20.69	0.00	0.00	100.00
One	18.04	0.00	0.00	100.00
Two	10.46	0.00	0.00	75.00
More than Two	22.38	0.00	0.00	100.00

Table 6.4.1 Funding from all other sources

	Mean	Median	Minimum	Maximum
Entire sample	8.18	0.00	0.00	100.00

Table 6.4.2 Funding from all other sources, Broken out by law school ranking

Law school ranking	Mean	Median	Minimum	Maximum
Top 20	38.00	0.00	0.00	100.00
20 - 50	0.00	0.00	0.00	0.00
51 - 80	2.73	0.00	0.00	30.00
81 - 100	6.89	0.00	0.00	40.00
101 - 150	4.50	0.00	0.00	25.00
More than 150	15.00	0.00	0.00	90.00

Table 6.4.3 Funding from all other sources, Broken out by Academic Title

Academic Title	Mean	Median	Minimum	Maximum
Professor	7.41	0.00	0.00	100.00
Assistant/Associate Professor/Lecturer or Research Fellow	0.00	0.00	0.00	0.00
Adjunct/Clinical Faculty	22.50	0.00	0.00	90.00
Emeritus	0.00	0.00	0.00	0.00
Staff and Administration	30.00	0.00	0.00	90.00

Table 6.4.4 Funding from all other sources, Broken out by age of survey respondent

Age of survey respondent	Mean	Median	Minimum	Maximum
30-39	0.00	0.00	0.00	0.00
40-49	16.25	12.50	0.00	40.00
50-59	9.38	0.00	0.00	100.00
60 or Over	6.73	0.00	0.00	90.00

Table 6.4.5 Funding from all other sources, Broken out by gender of the survey participant

Gender of the survey participant	Mean	Median	Minimum	Maximum
Male	7.94	0.00	0.00	100.00
Female	8.61	0.00	0.00	90.00

Table 6.4.6 Funding from all other sources, Broken out by law school enrollment

Law school enrolment	Mean	Median	Minimum	Maximum
Less than 500	6.00	0.00	0.00	90.00
500 - 600	1.69	0.00	0.00	25.00
601 - 1000	16.67	0.00	0.00	90.00
More than 1000	12.50	0.00	0.00	100.00

Table 6.4.7 Funding from all other sources, Broken out for public and private universities

Is your law school public or private?	Mean	Median	Minimum	Maximum
Public	4.33	0.00	0.00	90.00
Private	13.67	0.00	0.00	100.00

Table 6.4.8 All Other Broken out by in the past semester how many courses did you teach?

In the past semester how many courses did you teach?	Mean	Median	Minimum	Maximum
None	10.00	0.00	0.00	90.00
One	17.50	0.00	0.00	100.00
Two	1.25	0.00	0.00	25.00
More than Two	3.67	0.00	0.00	20.00

In which subject areas and from which institutional sources do you feel that funding is likely to increase and in which areas is it likely to decline? Broken out by law school ranking

Top 20

1) no idea
2) No opinion
3) Constitutional law
4) Increase in experiential
5) NA

20 - 50

1) Our own university and private sector foundations may increase. I see little reason for federal government funding to increase
2) Don't know
3) increase = business law decrease = criminal law and other poverty initiatives
4) I don't seek grants so I don't know.
5) No opinion.
6) N/A. See above, limited support for clinical faculty
7) Criminal law - All govt and private foundations Family law - state govt and foundations Dispute Resolution - All govts, foundations
8) Whoever wrote this survey doesn't seem to know/understand that there are virtually no grants in legal research, legal research is seldom grant-driven, and there is essentially no culture or infrastructure for grant applications in law schools.
9) International business and arbitration.
10) The hot area seems to be around the general, and fairly undefined, "artificial intelligence" and "algorithmic bias"
11) Don't know
12) Law relative to financial transactions and natural resources will likely increase. Do not see an area of decrease.

51 - 80

1) n/a
2) Arts & Culture, Technology will increase
3) More NSF for law, more foundation
4) Digital media;
5) increase - student financial aid decrease - library
6) don't know
7) Don't know

8) No idea
9) Unsure
10) STEM
11) increase in sciences and decrease in arts
12) intellectual property and privacy
13) More private foundations
14) Alumni Donor support

81 - 100

1) I don't know. I am a clinical professor of law, so these issues are irrelevant for me.
2) Law school funding appears to be likely to decline.
3) NA
4) All outside source grant funding will have to increase for law schools to remain sustainable. I anticipate it will begin to model undergraduate institutions that rely heavily on grant funding. The legal academy has never had to do this so is coming in late in the game with little knowledge of sources of funding.
5) No opinion
6) Increasingly Trade and development (Fed), Immigration Decline: Criminal Law
7) Increases in labor & employment law and intellectual property. Decreases across the board for most other areas.
8) Law school research funding is currently threatened by University financial difficulties.
9) Scientific and empirical research will increase.
10) Criminal law policy
11) Unknown

101 - 150

1) Environmental Law and Experiential Law funding
2) University funding for standard law faculty research is minimal and is apt to remain so. If funding from the law school remains constant with 2019, that would be a plus.
3) n/a
4) None
5) None
6) Tuition Increase from the University Scholarship Decrease

More than 150

1) unknown
2) NA

3) Federal grants
4) I have no idea
5) Our university has no mechanism for looking for outside funding. Some faculty stumble upon grant opportunities on their own. That's about it.

Table 7.1 How many grants have you applied for within the past 12 months?

	Mean	Median	Minimum	Maximum
Entire sample	1.26	0.00	0.00	12.00

Table 7.2 How many grants have you applied for within the past 12 months? Broken out by law school ranking

Law school ranking	Mean	Median	Minimum	Maximum
Top 20	2.09	0.00	0.00	10.00
20 - 50	0.80	0.00	0.00	4.00
51 - 80	1.15	0.00	0.00	10.00
81 - 100	0.60	0.00	0.00	3.00
101 - 150	2.40	0.50	0.00	12.00
More than 150	0.33	0.00	0.00	1.00

Table 7.3 How many grants have you applied for within the past 12 months? Broken out by Academic Title

Academic Title	Mean	Median	Minimum	Maximum
Professor	1.13	0.00	0.00	12.00
Assistant/Associate Professor/Lecturer or Research Fellow	0.60	0.00	0.00	6.00
Adjunct/Clinical Faculty	2.13	1.00	0.00	10.00
Emeritus	0.80	0.00	0.00	4.00
Staff and Administration	3.00	1.00	0.00	10.00

Table 7.4 How many grants have you applied for within the past 12 months? Broken out by age of survey respondent

Age of survey respondent	Mean	Median	Minimum	Maximum
30-39	3.00	2.00	0.00	10.00
40-49	2.50	2.50	0.00	5.00
50-59	1.11	0.00	0.00	10.00
60 or Over	0.97	0.00	0.00	12.00

Table 7.5 How many grants have you applied for within the past 12 months? Broken out by gender of the survey participant

Gender of the survey participant	Mean	Median	Minimum	Maximum
Male	1.10	0.00	0.00	12.00
Female	1.50	0.50	0.00	10.00

Table 7.6 How many grants have you applied for within the past 12 months? Broken out by law school enrollment

Law school enrollment	Mean	Median	Minimum	Maximum
Less than 500	0.50	0.00	0.00	2.00
500 - 600	1.38	0.00	0.00	10.00
601 - 1000	1.47	0.00	0.00	12.00
More than 1000	1.46	0.00	0.00	10.00

Table 7.7 How many grants have you applied for within the past 12 months? Broken out for public and private universities

Is your law school public or private?	Mean	Median	Minimum	Maximum
Public	0.90	0.00	0.00	12.00
Private	1.56	0.00	0.00	10.00

Table 7.8 How many grants have you applied for within the past 12 months? Broken out by in the past semester how many courses did you teach?

In the past semester how many courses did you teach?	Mean	Median	Minimum	Maximum
None	0.70	0.00	0.00	4.00
One	1.56	0.00	0.00	10.00
Two	0.74	0.00	0.00	5.00
More than Two	2.71	1.00	0.00	12.00

Table 8 Have you ever done any of the following? (check all that apply)

Table 8.1.1 Have you ever checked the law library collection for information about legal research funding?

	Yes	No
Entire sample	8.33%	91.67%

Table 8.1.2 Have you ever checked the law library collection for information about legal research funding? Broken out by law school ranking

Law school ranking	Yes	No
Top 20	8.33%	91.67%
20 - 50	0.00%	100.00%
51 - 80	5.00%	95.00%
81 - 100	0.00%	100.00%
101 - 150	21.05%	78.95%
More than 150	18.18%	81.82%

Table 8.1.3 Have you ever checked the law library collection for information about legal research funding? Broken out by Academic Title

You are:	Yes	No
Professor	9.62%	90.38%
Assistant/Associate Professor/Lecturer or Research Fellow	0.00%	100.00%
Adjunct/Clinical Faculty	7.14%	92.86%
Emeritus	0.00%	100.00%
Staff and Administration	25.00%	75.00%

Table 8.1.4 Have you ever checked the law library collection for information about legal research funding? Broken out by age of survey respondent

How old are you	Yes	No
30-39	0.00%	100.00%
40-49	11.11%	88.89%
50-59	11.54%	88.46%
60 or Over	7.41%	92.59%

Table 8.1.5 Have you ever checked the law library collection for information about legal research funding? Broken out by gender of the survey participant

Are you male or female?	Yes	No
Male	11.86%	88.14%
Female	2.70%	97.30%

Table 8.1.6 Have you ever checked the law library collection for information about legal research funding? Broken out by law school enrollment

Your law school has approximately how many students?	Yes	No
Less than 500	8.70%	91.30%
500 - 600	14.29%	85.71%
601 - 1000	7.69%	92.31%
More than 1000	0.00%	100.00%

Table 8.1.7 Have you ever checked the law library collection for information about legal research funding? Broken out for public and private universities

Is your law school public or private?	Yes	No
Public	4.35%	95.65%
Private	12.00%	88.00%

Table 8.1.8 Have you ever checked the law library collection for information about legal research funding? Broken out by in the past semester how many courses did you teach?

In the past semester how many courses did you teach?	Yes	No
None	9.52%	90.48%
One	2.94%	97.06%
Two	9.68%	90.32%
More than Two	20.00%	80.00%

Table 8.2.1 Have you ever checked the general university library for information about legal research funding?

	Yes	No
Entire sample	4.17%	95.83%

Table 8.2.2 Have you ever checked the general university library for information about legal research funding? Broken out by law school ranking

Law school ranking	Yes	No
Top 20	0.00%	100.00%
20 - 50	10.53%	89.47%
51 - 80	5.00%	95.00%
81 - 100	0.00%	100.00%
101 - 150	5.26%	94.74%
More than 150	0.00%	100.00%

Table 8.2.3 Have you ever checked the general university library for information about legal research funding? Broken out by Academic Title

You are:	Yes	No
Professor	5.77%	94.23%
Assistant/Associate Professor/Lecturer or Research Fellow	0.00%	100.00%
Adjunct/Clinical Faculty	0.00%	100.00%
Emeritus	14.29%	85.71%
Staff and Administration	0.00%	100.00%

Table 8.2.4 Have you ever checked the general university library for information about legal research funding? Broken out by age of survey respondent

How old are you	Yes	No
30-39	0.00%	100.00%
40-49	0.00%	100.00%
50-59	3.85%	96.15%
60 or Over	5.56%	94.44%

Table 8.2.5 Have you ever checked the general university library for information about legal research funding? Broken out by gender of the survey participant

Are you male or female?	Yes	No
Male	6.78%	93.22%
Female	0.00%	100.00%

Table 8.2.6 Have you ever checked the general university library for information about legal research funding? Broken out by law school enrollment

Your law school has approximately how many students?	Yes	No
Less than 500	0.00%	100.00%
500 - 600	7.14%	92.86%
601 - 1000	7.69%	92.31%
More than 1000	0.00%	100.00%

Table 8.2.7 Have you ever checked the general university library for information about legal research funding? Broken out for public and private universities

Is your law school public or private?	Yes	No
Public	4.35%	95.65%
Private	4.00%	96.00%

Table 8.2.8 Have you ever checked the general university library for information about legal research funding? Broken out by in the past semester how many courses did you teach?

In the past semester how many courses did you teach?	Yes	No
None	9.52%	90.48%
One	0.00%	100.00%
Two	3.23%	96.77%
More than Two	10.00%	90.00%

Table 8.3.1 Have you ever used a grants or funding database offered by the law library?

	Yes	No
Entire sample	6.25%	93.75%

Table 8.3.2 Have you ever used a grants or funding database offered by the law library? Broken out by law school ranking

Law school ranking	Yes	No
Top 20	0.00%	100.00%
20 - 50	10.53%	89.47%
51 - 80	10.00%	90.00%
81 - 100	0.00%	100.00%
101 - 150	5.26%	94.74%
More than 150	9.09%	90.91%

Table 8.3.3 Have you ever used a grants or funding database offered by the law library? Broken out by Academic Title

You are:	Yes	No
Professor	7.69%	92.31%
Assistant/Associate Professor/Lecturer or Research Fellow	0.00%	100.00%
Adjunct/Clinical Faculty	7.14%	92.86%
Emeritus	0.00%	100.00%
Staff and Administration	12.50%	87.50%

Table 8.3.4 Have you ever used a grants or funding database offered by the law library? Broken out by age of survey respondent

How old are you	Yes	No
30-39	14.29%	85.71%
40-49	11.11%	88.89%
50-59	7.69%	92.31%
60 or Over	3.70%	96.30%

Table 8.3.5 Have you ever used a grants or funding database offered by the law library? Broken out by gender of the survey participant

Are you male or female?	Yes	No
Male	5.08%	94.92%
Female	8.11%	91.89%

Table 8.3.6 Have you ever used a grants or funding database offered by the law library? Broken out by law school enrollment

Your law school has approximately how many students?	Yes	No
Less than 500	0.00%	100.00%
500 - 600	7.14%	92.86%
601 - 1000	11.54%	88.46%
More than 1000	5.26%	94.74%

Table 8.3.7 Have you ever used a grants or funding database offered by the law library? Broken out for public and private universities

Is your law school public or private?	Yes	No
Public	4.35%	95.65%
Private	8.00%	92.00%

Table 8.3.8 Have you ever used a grants or funding database offered by the law library? Broken out by in the past semester how many courses did you teach?

In the past semester how many courses did you teach?	Yes	No
None	4.76%	95.24%
One	8.82%	91.18%
Two	6.45%	93.55%
More than Two	0.00%	100.00%

Table 8.4.1 Have you ever used a grants or funding database offered by the general university library?

	Yes	No
Entire sample	11.46%	88.54%

Table 8.4.2 Have you ever used a grants or funding database offered by the general university library? Broken out by law school ranking

Law school ranking	Yes	No
Top 20	8.33%	91.67%
20 - 50	26.32%	73.68%
51 - 80	15.00%	85.00%
81 - 100	6.67%	93.33%
101 - 150	0.00%	100.00%
More than 150	9.09%	90.91%

Table 8.4.3 Have you ever used a grants or funding database offered by the general university library? Broken out by Academic Title

You are:	Yes	No
Professor	13.46%	86.54%
Assistant/Associate Professor/Lecturer or Research Fellow	6.67%	93.33%
Adjunct/Clinical Faculty	14.29%	85.71%
Emeritus	14.29%	85.71%
Staff and Administration	0.00%	100.00%

Table 8.4.4 Have you ever used a grants or funding database offered by the general university library? Broken out by age of survey respondent

How old are you	Yes	No
30-39	28.57%	71.43%
40-49	0.00%	100.00%
50-59	15.38%	84.62%
60 or Over	9.26%	90.74%

Table 8.4.5 Have you ever used a grants or funding database offered by the general university library? Broken out by gender of the survey participant

Are you male or female?	Yes	No
Male	11.86%	88.14%
Female	10.81%	89.19%

Table 8.4.6 Have you ever used a grants or funding database offered by the general university library? Broken out by law school enrollment

Your law school has approximately how many students?	Yes	No
Less than 500	4.35%	95.65%
500 - 600	10.71%	89.29%
601 - 1000	15.38%	84.62%
More than 1000	15.79%	84.21%

Table 8.4.7 Have you ever used a grants or funding database offered by the general university library? Broken out for public and private universities

Is your law school public or private?	Yes	No
Public	19.57%	80.43%
Private	4.00%	96.00%

Table 8.4.8 Have you ever used a grants or funding database offered by the general university library? Broken out by in the past semester how many courses did you teach?

In the past semester how many courses did you teach?	Yes	No
None	19.05%	80.95%
One	11.76%	88.24%
Two	9.68%	90.32%
More than Two	0.00%	100.00%

Table 8.5.1 Have you ever used a grants or funding database offered by the research office of the law school or general university?

	Yes	No
Entire sample	11.46%	88.54%

Table 8.5.2 Have you ever used a grants or funding database offered by the research office of the law school or general university? Broken out by law school ranking

Law school ranking	Yes	No
Top 20	0.00%	100.00%
20 - 50	21.05%	78.95%
51 - 80	25.00%	75.00%
81 - 100	6.67%	93.33%
101 - 150	5.26%	94.74%
More than 150	0.00%	100.00%

Table 8.5.3 Have you ever used a grants or funding database offered by the research office of the law school or general university? Broken out by Academic Title

You are:	Yes	No
Professor	11.54%	88.46%
Assistant/Associate Professor/Lecturer or Research Fellow	6.67%	93.33%
Adjunct/Clinical Faculty	14.29%	85.71%
Emeritus	14.29%	85.71%
Staff and Administration	12.50%	87.50%

Table 8.5.4 Have you ever used a grants or funding database offered by the research office of the law school or general university? Broken out by age of survey respondent

How old are you	Yes	No
30-39	28.57%	71.43%
40-49	33.33%	66.67%
50-59	7.69%	92.31%
60 or Over	7.41%	92.59%

Table 8.5.5 Have you ever used a grants or funding database offered by the research office of the law school or general university? Broken out by gender of the survey participant

Are you male or female?	Yes	No
Male	8.47%	91.53%
Female	16.22%	83.78%

Table 8.5.6 Have you ever used a grants or funding database offered by the research office of the law school or general university? Broken out by law school enrollment

Your law school has approximately how many students?	Yes	No
Less than 500	0.00%	100.00%
500 - 600	17.86%	82.14%
601 - 1000	19.23%	80.77%
More than 1000	5.26%	94.74%

Table 8.5.7 Have you ever used a grants or funding database offered by the research office of the law school or general university? Broken out for public and private universities

Is your law school public or private?	Yes	No
Public	6.52%	93.48%
Private	16.00%	84.00%

Table 8.5.8 Have you ever used a grants or funding database offered by the research office of the law school or general university? Broken out by in the past semester how many courses did you teach?

In the past semester how many courses did you teach?	Yes	No
None	9.52%	90.48%
One	11.76%	88.24%
Two	16.13%	83.87%
More than Two	0.00%	100.00%

What can your research office or library do to better assist you in searching for and obtaining grants to support your research? Broken out by law school ranking

Top 20

1) Match my areas of interest and expertise to existing funding sources
2) Continue to compile relevant grants and provide this information with a lot of lead time.
3) NA

20 - 50

1) Send targeted emails to faculty with information about grants that might be relevant to each individual faculty member.
2) Don't know
3) Uncertain
4) We have an excellent library staff when it comes to seeking grants -- at least this is what my colleagues tell me.
5) No assistance needed
6) I'm not looking.
7) Advocate for research and support funding for clinics!
8) Librarians could identify particular governmental funding sources for particular areas - e.g. criminal justice; family-law issues, etc. University/College development/research has been helpful in re-writing drafts - but of no value in identifying possible resources.
9) please see comment above
10) n/a

51 - 80

1) First, send notice of grants to me.
2) more grant writing assistance, though hard to do if not engaged in the program work
3) Find sources and funding rfps
4) -
5) I am retiring so there is not much I need.
6) Hold a workshop in which people actually apply for the grants
7) Unsure
8) targeted emails with opportunities
9) Hiring a grant support person
10) Hire a full -time person to help with grant writing.
11) na

81 - 100

1) n/a
2) Training my administrative assistant to help with finding and obtaining grants.
3) NA
4) Anything. We have no information on grant funding or sources or any knowledge of where to look. I know of one clinic that applied and received grant funding, but to my knowledge, few other faculty members have received grant funding.
5) Let us know about law specific grants.
6) Know something,have integrity
7) Not Applicable
8) Locate grant opportunities and pursue them.
9) Letting me know of possible grants opportunities related to my office.
10) More proactive research on potential funding sources.
11) N/A

101 - 150

1) Legal Innovation grants are not our focus - Environmental grants are. I'd like to see a broader look at the possibilities.
2) Be proactive in informing law faculty of new opportunities apt to be of interest.
3) Talk about it
4) Give me more time to research it
5) There is no one currently performing the function of assisting faculty with research grants, and with rare exception, there never has been.
6) We have no research office
7) Educate us about the process and available services

More than 150

1) unknown
2) training
3) NA
4) communicate resources
5) I am not sure.
6) Create any of the databases listed above

What are some of the best or emerging sources of support for legal research funding? Broken out by law school ranking

Top 20

1) Foundations
2) Private sector
3) Foundations
4) NA

20 - 50

1) Don't know
2) Don't know
3) Uncertain
4) n/a
5) National Security Law, Cybersecurity
6) I don't know.
7) Criminal law; 'urban unrest'; family; environmental; judicial reform;
8) please see comment above
9) Little experience.

51 - 80

1) Arts & Culture
2) Alphabet, Apple, Facebook.
3) I have no idea
4) Don't know.
5) Unsure
6) ABA Foundation
7) ukn

81 - 100

1) I don't know.
2) Don't know.
3) NA
4) I do not know.
5) No opinion
6) Politicized foundations, Right or Left
7) Reaching out to private corporations in Chicago area
8) NSF, AccessLex.
9) N/A

101 - 150

1) Cross over grants with other disciplines.
2) I don't know.
3) IDK
4) The surviving Koch brother is giving out money, but there's no way I'd take it
5) Alumni that feel their money is going towards things that will make a future stamp at the law school.

More than 150

1) unknown
2) NA
3) volunteer grant writer
4) I do not know.
5) I have no idea

Made in the USA
Middletown, DE
03 November 2026

36496627R00051